Spelling Succe
-HOMOPHONES
by
Chris Blance and Philip Cooper.

ACKNOWLEGEMENTS.

The following pupils of mine are all using the mnemonic spelling system;

Gregory W. Hannah S. Neil G. Lucy N. Tom T. Alex C. Christopher W.
Katheryn C. Walton S. Sarah N. Mark E. William A. Alan T. Stephen M.
Lauren B. Gemma T. Christopher R. Mathew B. Ian S. Jamie D. Philip S.
Daniel G. Leigh D. Tammy D. Hilary B. Patrick B. Cheryl A. David N.
David H. Charlotte H. Gareth R. Daniel D. Danny H. Louise S. Claire B.
Debbie B. Adam B. Sean B. Stephen E. Mark R. Linsey F. Donna F.
Tracy F. Mark G. Tony M. Gregory H Andrew S. Richard W. Timothy D.
Ilona F. Dominic B. Stephanie B. Faye S. Carl E. Chris B. Stephen R.
Robbie M. Aran F. Mathew W. Chloe W. Jake C William B. Anna G.
Simon T. Daniel A. Zoe M. Rose B. Ally S. Peter P. Kayleigh R. Bryn S
Laura T. Sam C. Tom W. Nicky W. Claire T Sean B. Mathew N.
Harriet A. Zoe K.Jason W. Oliver N.

Published 1999 by Help for Dyslexia

Second Edition 2020

MNEMONIC SPELLING SYSTEM

INTRODUCTION

Searching for a way to help a pupil of mine retain in her memory the spelling of high frequency words, I remembered from my University days the value of mnemonics. Spelling words using mnemonics is not original. Many pupils are taught awkward words like "because" and "said" by this method. However, what about the hundreds of other high frequency words which cause problems? Filling a pupil`s head with hundreds of separate mnemonics would cause confusion-unless the mnemonic begins with the word itself. This is where I believe my method is unique and it also accounts for its success rate.

Hundreds of pupils over nearly five years have been using this particular method, many with amazing results.At present one pupil has learned and retained over 400 chant spellings, several have 200 and many have over 100.

The gains achieved in spelling ability are matched by gains in confidence and self esteem which have been remarked upon by other teachers.

HOMOPHONES

As homophones are words which sound exactly the same but which have both different spelling and meaning, the problem is more complex. Mnemonics are an ideal tool to overcome this confusion because they lock both the meaning and spelling into the memory.

ie. **bread** is memorised by **bread rolls eaten at dinner**

   bred is memorised by **bred really exotic dogs.**

HOW IT WORKS

read	read every available dictionary	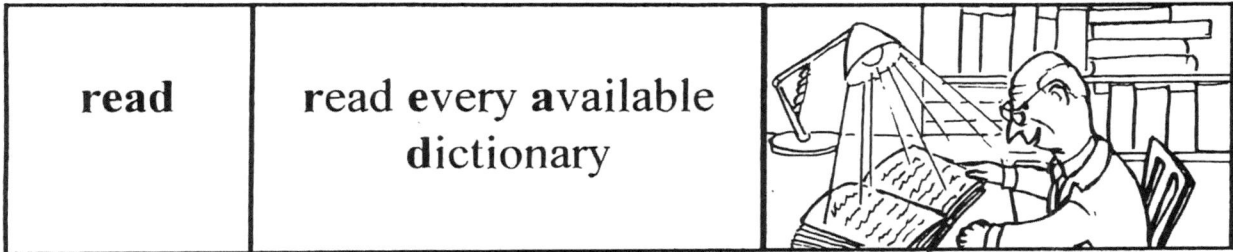

Quite simply each word has its own mnemonic and a cartoon picture. The picture and mnemonic capture the context of the word, bringing it alive. By repeating the mnemonic a few times, the spelling of the word is usually fixed in the mind.

E.G; read every available dictionary.

r　　e　　a　　d

To recall the spelling, simply repeat the mnemonic chant.

HOW TO USE THESE CHANTS.
1. Working from the word list (Achievement Record) supplied with this book, carry out a test and mark words incorrectly spelt.
2. Target a few of these words at a time.
3. Learn the chant for each word by repeating it out loud.
(You do not need to write out the chants.)

HOW TO MONITOR PROGRESS.
1. Keep a check on how many chants are known.
2. Add a few new ones every day.
3. With a partner, test your chants out loud.
4. Have frequent spelling tests and monitor your progress on the Achievment Record sheet.
5. Certificates can be awarded for every 50 learned (using the master copy provided).

INCREASING THE SPEED OF THE CHANTS.

1. On reaching a certain number, test your speed with a stop-watch. Note the time.
2. At each practice session attempt to beat your own record!

OTHER APPLICATIONS OF THE MNEMONICS.
Although originally created as a spelling aid for school pupils, these mnemonics of homophones are also helpful in improving Adult Literacy as well as English as a Second Language.
With all pupils the use of mnemonics helps to expand memory and increase self esteem.

Chris Blance 1999

ENDORSEMENTS.
Homophones have always been a problem to me, but since I have been learning about them, they don`t bother me any more. This method has been a great help to me and my school work. I am sure it will be for a long time. Gregory W.(17)

Homophones help me spell, they also help to tell me the difference between a word that sounds the same but is spelled differently. I know 64 homophones and I use them wherever I go. They are planted in my head! Hannah S. (12)

When I hear the word, a really vivid picture leaps into my mind-helping me to spell the word. This helps me choose the right one. Neil G. (12)

The chants for homophones have helped me a lot at school. When I have to decide which spelling, the chant gives me a clue. Lucy N. (10)

ate	ate ten eggs	
eight	eight Indians go hunting tonight	
ball	ball among large lads	
bawl	bawl at wealthy lady	
bare	bare actress runs everywhere	
bear	bear eats a recorder	

beach	**b**each **e**xplorer **a**dmires **c**rabs **h**ere	
beech	**b**eech **e**asily **e**ncloses **c**hildren`s **h**ut	
blew	**bl**ew **l**eaves,**e**mptying **w**heelbarrow	
blue	**bl**ue **l**ips **u**pon **E**mma	
boar	**b**oar **o**ften **a**ttacks **r**ats	
bore	**b**ore **o**ld **R**onnie **e**ndlessly	

(pg1)

axe

kate

gight

eight

bdall

dbawl

~~bark~~

Wball

bawl

behar

bared

barea

~~betar~~

(pg2)

bebahc

beiccn

bewb

blue

boar

bore

board	board **on a** red **d**oor	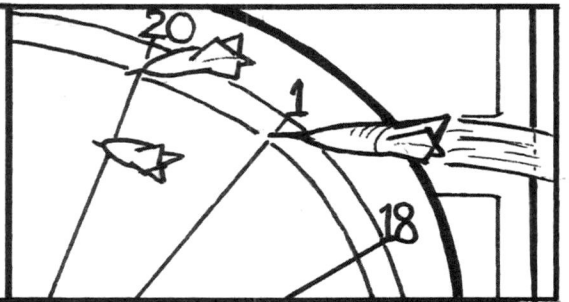
bored	**b**ored **o**ld **R**onnie **e**ventually **d**ies	
boarder	**b**oarder **o**ccupies **a** **r**oom **d**rinking **e**xpensive **r**um	
border	**b**order **of r**ed **d**ahlias **e**ventually **r**otted	
bough	**b**ough **of u**nusually **g**reat **h**awthorn	
bow	**b**ow **of w**aiter	

boy	**boy** often yells	
buoy	**buoy under orange yacht**	
brake	**brake really abruptly - kitten`s escaped**	
break	**break really expensive antique kettle**	
bread	**bread rolls eaten at dinner**	
bred	**bred really exotic dogs**	

© 1999 C. Blance . P. Cooper

campers	campers are making puffins eat raw sausages	
campus	campus attracts many pompous university students	
caught	caught an unusually green hedgehog today	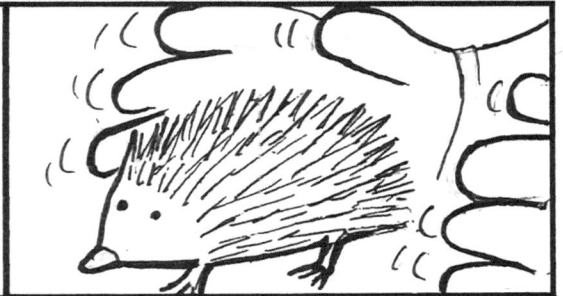
court	court official upsets royal teenager	
check	check hotel's extremely clean kitchen	
cheque	cheque has eleven quid unclearly entered	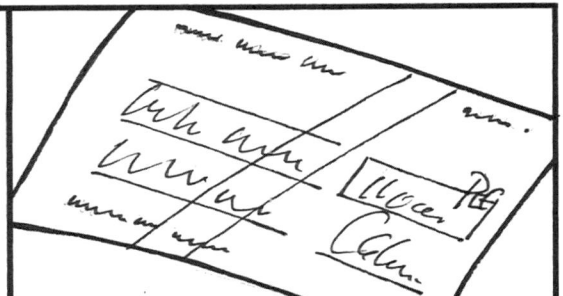

conker	**c**onker **o**f **n**ew **k**id **e**asily **r**olls	
conquer	**c**onquer **o**ld **n**ation-**q**ueen **u**sually **e**xpects **r**esults	
creak	**c**reak **r**egularly **e**xasperates **A**unty **K**athy	
creek	**c**reek **r**eally **e**ndangers **E**skimo`s **k**ayak	
currants	**c**urrants **u**sually **r**esemble **r**aisins **and** **n**ot **t**iny **s**ultanas	
currents	**c**urrents **u**nder **r**ushing **r**iver **e**xhaust **n**ine **t**errified **s**wimmers	

© 1999 C. Blance . P.Cooper

dear	"Dear Edward and Rita"	
deer	deer eats every rose	
die	die in Egypt	
dye	dye yellow eggs	
done	done only nine exams	
dun	"Dun" uttered Nancy	

draw	draw round **a worm**	
drawer	drawer retains **a** womans exotic rings	
fair	fair **a**lways includes roundabouts	
fare	fare **a**nnoys rich Egyptian	
father	father **and** the **h**en enjoy running	
farther	farther **a**long road truck **has** entered river	

fined	fined Irish nun exporting drugs	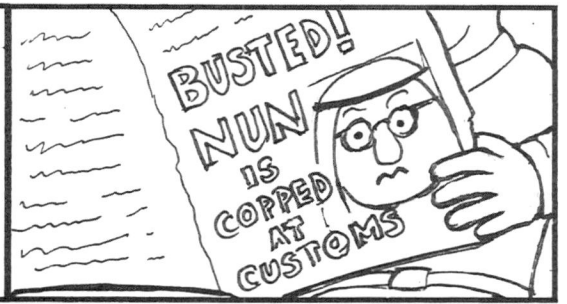
find	find ink near desk	
fir	fir interests rooks	
fur	fur upon Ruby	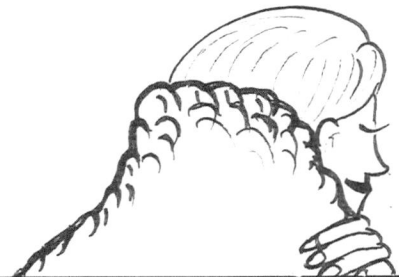
flea	flea leaps easily around	
flee	"Flee"-let everyone escape	

flower	flower lady offers woman exotic roses	
flour	flour leaks on Uncle`s rug	
foul	foul ointment upsets lady	
fowl	fowl on wooden log	
gamble	gamble away my brothers large earnings	
gambol	gambol across meadow:boy observes lambs	

gorilla	gorilla **on** road **is** leaving litter **about**	
guerilla	guerilla **u**sually **e**mits rowdy instructions leading large **ar**my	
grate	grate **r**usts **at** the edges	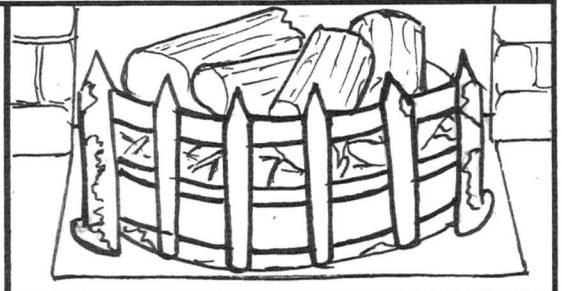
great	great **r**oyal emperor **a**dmires treasure	
groan	groan **r**eally **of**ten **ab**out **n**eighbours	
grown	grown **r**eally **o**dd whiskers **n**ow	

guest	guest unpacks every skirt tenderly	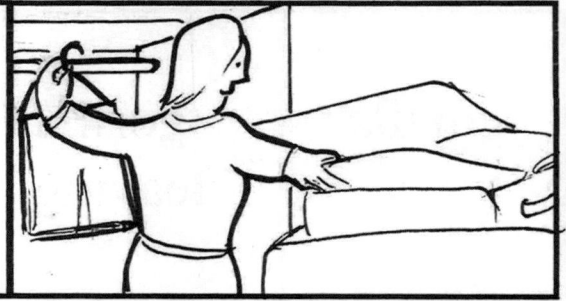
guessed	guessed Uncle Edward's secret so easily, dear	
hail	hail alarms Indian lady	
hale	"Hale a lad, Edgar"	
hair	hair appears incredibly red	
hare	hare and rabbits eat	

hangar	**h**angar **at n**oon gives **a**eroplane **r**oom	
hanger	**h**anger **a**ccommodates **n**ew **g**uest`s **e**xotic **r**obes	
heal	**h**eal **e**very **a**ching limb	
heel	**h**eel **e**levates **e**lderly lady	
hear	**h**ear **e**normous **a**ligator **r**oar	
here	**h**ere **E**ddy **r**eads **e**verything	

heard	**h**eard **e**very **a**nnoying **r**abbit **d**rumming	
herd	**h**erd **e**merged **r**ound **d**oorway	
higher	**h**igher **i**nto **g**reat **h**ills **e**veryone **r**uns	
hire	**h**ire **i**t **r**eally **e**arly	
him	"**H**im" **I** **m**uttered	
hymn	**h**ymn **y**ields **m**usical **n**otes	

hoarse	**h**oarse **o**ld **a**ctor **r**ecites sonnets **e**verywhere	
horse	**h**orse **o**ften **r**uns **so** **e**agerly	
hole	**h**ole **on** lawn **e**xpands	
whole	**w**hole **h**ippo **o**ften **l**ooks **e**normous	
in	"**In**, **n**ow!"	
Inn	**Inn** **n**ear **N**ewcastle	

lessen	lessen existing savings; spend everything now	
lesson	lesson excites some sweet old nuns	
loch	loch overflows causing havoc	
lock	lock on cook's kitchen	
made	made a daring escape	
maid	maid appears in doorway	

main	**m**ain **a**ttraction in Newcastle	
mane	**m**ane **a**ppears **n**ever ending	
manner	**m**anner **an**noys **n**ice **n**urse **e**ntering **r**oom	
manor	**m**anor **a**ppears **n**eglected **o**n **r**oof	
marshall	**m**arshall **a**rrests **r**owdy soccer hooligans **a**long long lane	
martial	**m**artial **a**rts **r**eally tempts incredibly **a**ngry lady	

© 1999 C. Blance . P.Cooper

matted	**m**atted **a**nimal tried to enter **d**oorway	
mattered	**m**attered about **the** **tw**ins **e**ating **r**ubbish every **d**ay	
meat	**m**eat eaters **a**t table	
meet	**m**eet **E**lizabeth **E**dwards today	
miner	**m**iner **i**s **n**ow **e**xcavating **r**ubies	
minor	**m**inor incident never occurred **r**eally	

muscle	**m**uscle **up**on shoulder **c**an look **e**normous	
mussel	**m**ussel **u**nder slimey shore **eats** little	
naval	**n**aval **a**viator visits **a** lady	
navel	**n**avel, **a**lways **v**isible, **e**xcites lads	
night	**n**ight in **g**hostly **h**ouse tonight	
knight	**k**night **n**early injured grey **h**orse`s **t**ail	

none	**n**one **of** N**ed**'s **escaped**	
nun	**n**un **up**set **N**anna	
hour	**h**our **of u**nbearable **r**unning	
our	**our** U**ncle**'s **r**oom	
pail	**p**ail **a**ccumulates **i**cy liquid	
pale	**p**ale **a**nimal **l**ooks **ee**rie	

pain	**p**ain **a**fter inserting **n**eedle	
pane	**p**ane **at n**ew **e**ntrance	
peal	**p**eal **e**xcites **A**bbey ladies	
peel	**p**eel **e**very **e**normous lemon	
pedal	**p**edal **e**very **d**ay **a**long lanes	
peddle	"**P**eddle **e**very **d**uster, **D**oreen-look **e**ager"	

© 1999 C. Blance . P.Cooper

presence	**p**resence **r**adiates **e**nergy; singer **e**mits **n**otes **c**ausing explosions	
presents	**p**resents **r**eally **e**xcited **S**anta **e**ntering **n**ew **t**oy shop	
prophet	**p**rophet **r**eads **o**n-**p**reaching **h**is **e**xcellent texts	
profit	**p**rofit **r**ises **o**n **f**abrics, **i**mpressing **t**raders	
put	**p**ut **u**p **t**en	
putt	**p**utt **u**nder **t**all **t**rees	

read	**r**ead **e**very **a**vailable dictionary	
red	**r**ed **e**arrings **d**angle	
role	**r**ole **o**ffers **l**ady **e**xperience	
roll	**r**oll **o**ver **l**arge **l**abrador	
root	**r**oot **o**f **o**ld **t**ree	
route	**r**oute **o**f **u**nderground train ends	

sail	sail **a**cross **i**cy lake	
sale	sale **a**t **l**arge exhibition	
sea	sea **e**xcites Aunty	
see	see **e**lephants **e**verywhere	
scene	scene **c**auses **e**xplorer **n**ew excitement	
seen	seen **e**ating **e**very **n**ut	

© 1999 C. Blance . P.Cooper

sent	sent exciting news today	
scent	scent confused elderly neighbours terrier	
ceiling	ceiling entertains Italian lady in new gallery	
sealing	sealing envelopes, always licking; it`s never good	
seams	seams extend around my shoulder	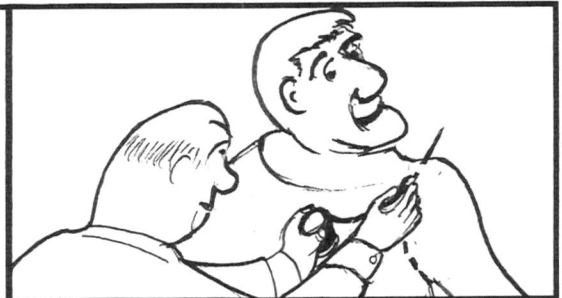
seems	seems extremely easy making scones	

sell	sell every lovely lettuce	
cell	cell encloses large lout	
side	side is dented everywhere	
sighed	sighed inwardly, grooming her enormous dog	
sighs	sighs in girls High School	
size	"Size it Zak- exactly"	

some	some **o**ld **m**onkey **e**xplodes	
sum	sum **u**psets **m**other	
son	son **of** Nigel	
sun	sun **u**mbrella **n**eeded	
stair	stair treads **a**ppear incredibly **r**usty	
stare	stare **t**errifies **a r**obust explorer	

stake	stake terrier **at kitchen** entrance	
steak	steak tastes excellent **among kidneys**	
stalk	stalk tickles **a little** kitten	
stork	stork takes **off royal kid**	
steal	steal terribly expensive antique lamp	
steel	steel turbines emit electric light	

story	story teller on radio yesterday	
storey	storey towers over really enormous yard	
sundae	sundae-unusually nice desserts, attracting everyone	
Sunday	Sunday- usually nice day all year	
swat	swat wildly at tarantula	
swot	swot was often teased	

tail	tail **a**ppears **i**ncredibly **l**ong	
tale	tale **a**larms little **E**ddy	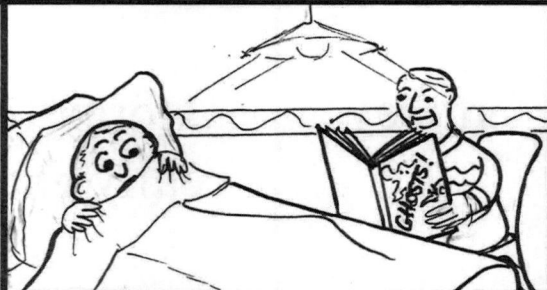
taught	taught **an** **u**ngrateful girl **h**istory today	
taut	taut **and** **u**nusually tense	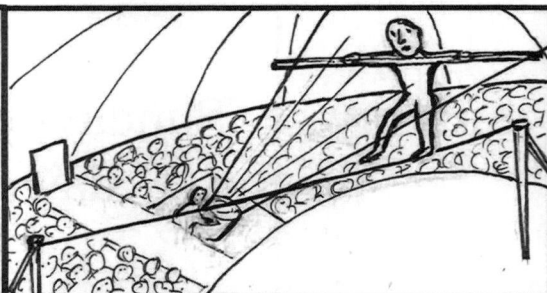
tears	tears **e**merge **and** **R**ita sobs	
tiers	tiers **i**nclude **e**dible **r**ed sugar	

their	their houses end in rows	
there	there he enjoys riding everywhere	
threw	threw his really enormous wellies	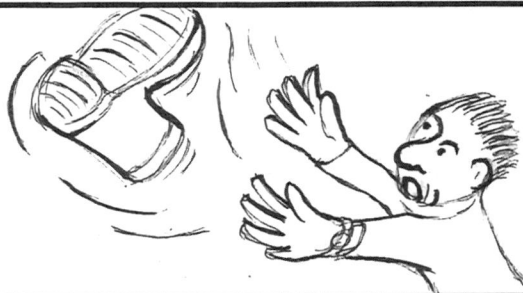
through	through his roof old Uncle goes home	
tire	tire in rotten exam	
tyre	tyre you repared exploded	

toad	toad **on a d**esk	
towed	towed **old** wagon every day	
toe	toe **of** elephant	
tow	tow old wagon	
earns	earns **a** really **ni**ce salary	
urns	**urns require new sprays**	

war	w**ar** **a**larms **r**eporter	
wore	**w**ore **o**ld **r**ed **e**arrings	
warn	**w**arn **a**bout **r**unning **n**aked	
worn	**w**orn **o**ld **r**ed **n**ightie	
weak	**w**eak **e**lephant **a**larms **k**eeper	
week	**w**eek **e**ntertaining **e**nergetic **k**ids	

wear	**w**ear expensive **a**ntique rings	
where	**w**here **h**ares **e**at, **r**abbits **e**at	
weather	**w**eather excited **a** toad; **h**e **e**njoys **r**ain	
whether	**w**hether **h**omesick **e**very **t**erm, **h**e **e**xpects **r**esults	
which	**w**hich **h**unter **i**s **c**oming **h**ome **?**	
witch	**w**itch **i**s **t**ickling **c**ats **h**ead	

whine	whine had irritated neighbours ears	
wine	wine is nearly empty	
one	one nasty eagle	
won	won only nine	
wood	wood on old door	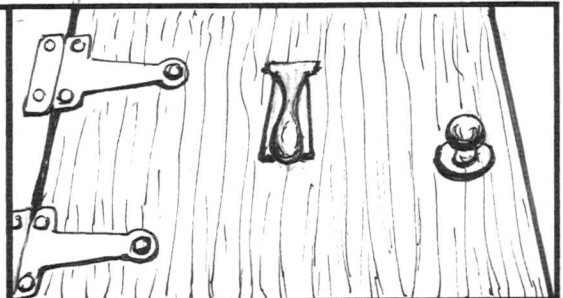
would	would old Uncle lie down	

by	by yourself	
bye	"Bye" yelled Emily	
buy	buy Uncle yoghurts	
pair	pair at Indian restaurant	
pare	pare away rough edge	
pear	pear eaten among rocks	

pause	pause abruptly under shop`s entrance	
paws	paws attacked white swan	
pores	pores on reptiles`s exotic skin	
rain	rain arrives in Nairobi	
reign	reign ends— it`s good news	
rein	rein eager infants now	

road	road often appears dangerous	
rode	rode old donkey everywhere	
rowed	rowed on water every day	
saw	saw a whale	
soar	soar over Abbey roof	
sore	sore on rabbits ear	

sew	sew **enormous waistcoat**	
so	so **old**	
sow	sow **only wheat**	
to	to **Oxford**	
too	"Too **orange Oliver!**"	
two	two **wise owls**	

ewe	**e**we **was e**normous	
yew	**y**ew **e**ndures **w**oodpecker	
you	**y**ou **o**ld **U**ncle	

Achievement Record.

Name——————————————

Date				Date				Date			
ate				31.conker				61.gorilla			
eight				32.conquer				62.guerilla			
ball				33.creak				63.grate			
bawl				34.creek				64.great			
bare				35.currants				65.groan			
bear				36.currents				66.grown			
beach				37.dear				67.guest			
beech				38.deer				68.guessed			
blew				39.die				69.hail			
.blue				40.dye				70.hale			
.boar				41.done				71.hair			
.bore				42.dun				72.hare			
.board				43.draw				73.hangar			
.bored				44.drawer				74.hanger			
.boarder				45.fair				75.heal			
.border				46.fare				76.heel			
.bough				47.father				77.hear			
.bow				48.farther				78.here			
.boy				49.fined				79.heard			
.buoy				50.find				80.herd			
.brake				51.fir				81.higher			
.break				52.fur				82.hire			
.bread				53.flea				83.him			
.bred				54.flee				84.hymn			
.campers				55.flower				85.hoarse			
.campus				56.flour				86.horse			
.caught				57.foul				87.hole			
.court				58.fowl				88.whole			
.check				59.gamble				89.in			
.cheque				60.gambol				90.Inn			

Name				Achievement Record.								

Date				Date				Date				
91.lessen				121.pain				151.sell				
92.lesson				122.pane				152.cell				
93.loch				123.peal				153.side				
94.lock				124.peel				154.sighed				
95.made				125.pedal				155.sighs				
96.maid				126.peddle				156.size				
97.main				127.prescence				157.some				
98.mane				128.presents				158.sum				
99.manner				129.prophet				159.son				
100.manor				130.profit				160.sun				
101.marshall				131.put				161stair				
102.martial				132.putt				162stare				
103.matted				133.read				163.stake				
104.mattered				134.red				164.steak				
105.meat				135.role				165.stalk				
106.meet				136.roll				166.stork				
107.miner				137.root				167.steal				
108.minor				138.route				168.steel				
109.muscle				139.sail				169.story				
110.mussel				140.sale				170.storey				
111.naval				141.sea				171.sundae				
112.navel				142.see				172.Sunday				
113.night				143.scene				173.swat				
114.knight				144.seen				174.swot				
115.none				145.sent				175.tail				
116.nun				146.scent				176.tale				
117.hour				147.ceiling				177.taught				
118.our				148.sealing				178.taut				
119.pail				149.seams				179.tears				
120.pale				150.seems				180.tiers				

Achievement Record.

te				Date				Date				
.their				211.by								
.there				212.bye								
.threw				213.buy								
.through				214.pair								
.tire				215.pare								
.tyre				216.pear								
.toad				217.pause								
.towed				218.paws								
.toe				219.pores								
,tow				220.rain								
.earns				221.reign								
.urns				222.rein								
.war				223.road								
.wore				224.rode								
.warn				225.rowed								
.worn				226.saw								
.weak				227.soar								
.week				228.sore								
.wear				229.sew								
.where				230.so								
.weather				231.sow.								
02.whether				232.to.								
03.which				233.too								
04.witch				234.two								
05.whine				235.ewe								
06.wine				236.yew								
07.one				237.you								
8.won												
09.wood												
10.would												

This is to certify that

_____

has reached the target of

_____

on _____

Congratulations !

signed by _____